THE LADDER
OF MEMORY

DAVID KOENIG

David Koenig

The Harp Song Press
Evanston, Illinois 60201

Library of Congress Catalog Card Number: 93-79443

Printed in the U.S.A.

10 9 8 7 6 5 4 3 2 1

ISBN: 0-9637357-0-5

ALSO BY DAVID KOENIG

Green Whistle (1988)

"The closest comparison...is to the works of Karl Shapiro and Denise Levertov. Distinguished company for a distinguished new poet."
-The Sentinel, Chicago

"[Koenig's] poems...find emotions and experiences that might be merely ordinary for other people. No trivial subjects here! [He] seems to find friends — and family — where others would not. It's an emotional universe...and that is good to come across in a world in many ways so chilly."
-John Frederick Nims, poet and
former editor of Poetry

"I was deeply moved by the tragic depths of [the] poems and by [the] craftsmanship...."
-Karl Shapiro
Pulitzer Prize for Poetry

"Resonant."
-Gwendolyn Brooks
Pulitzer Prize for Poetry

For Fritz and Else Goldstein, who survived and told their stories

For Fritz Koenig, my father, Lilly Koenig, my mother, Steven Koenig, my brother, Felice Koenig, my daughter, Louis Barlow, my stepson, and

For Joyce Koenig, my wife and editor

ACKNOWLEDGMENTS

Three of the poems collected here first appeared in the following publications: *The Rockford Review,* 1992 ("Menopause"), *Together,* Federation of Jewish Holocaust Survivors, 1992 ("Paper Rose") and *Wellsprings,* 1993 ("The Ladder of Memory"). I gratefully acknowledge Simon Wiesenthal ("Memory of an Interview"). I also acknowledge Theodor Kramer ("Ich Bin So Viel Zuhaus Und Bin Schon Nicht Mehr Hier" and "Wer Laeutet Draussen An Der Tuer?" from *Verbannt Aus Osterreich, Neue Gedichte*, Austrian P.E.N., London, 1943, reprinted by Hermann Bohlaus Nachf, Vienna, Cologne, Graz, 1983) from which the two translations in this book were made.

In Memory Of

Edmund Elias
Otto Raubitchek
Hanzi Raubitchek (age 13)
Grete Raubitchek
Ernst Zirner
Lotte Zirner

and relatives not known
who perished in the Holocaust
and all who were not relatives

(all victims are relatives)

TABLE OF CONTENTS

PHOTOGRAPHS

PART III—RETURN VISITS

TO GERMANY AND AUSTRIA

TWO TRANSLATIONS

SIMON WIESENTHAL

PART IV—HISTORICAL REFLECTIONS

MODERN PORTRAITS

ANCIENT PORTRAITS

PART V—THE PRESENT

TANTE ELSA IN THE GARDEN OF AMERICA

LADDERS

PART I

Mysteries

FATHER CODE

◪ CODED MESSAGES

Coded
Messages
Go out
From inside
A damaged heart,
Arrhythmic fits
And starts,

Systolic
And diastolic
Rhymes,
Ventricle
And auricle
Chimes,

Bluebells
And redbells
By turns,
Inhaling,
Expelling
Oxygen
Like ferns,

Giving off
Pollenated poetry
To the sun—
A wind-shaken,
Torn-petaled
Bloom,

Signaling
Unseen
And far off folk,
A cracked,
Ornately painted,
Ancient drum.

▦ ELECTRIC TRAIN

The surgeon whose hands
Could stroke skin
With a scalpel
Softly as a silent sigh,
Yet not the heads
Of his own boys,

Built an electric train set
In the attic on a table,
Not one track only
But paralleling itself
And tunneling back,
Sleek silver
And black locomotives,
Yellow freight cars,
Red caboose,
And real smoke coming out
The iron horse engine stack.

How our hearts would jump,
Our hands
On the black control box,
Mysterious as Father,
The bald man
Who could make our hearts
Start or stop,

How we raced with the trains
As they ran, and grieved
When they jumped track,
Questioning each other,
But never the bald man
With the thick German
Accent and frown,

In those American years
After the war,
Years when my boots shuffled
Miles of tracks in the snow,
Cold tunnels of a black heart
Making black tunnels in the cold.

◪ FATHER, THE POET

Would swallow
Great numbers
Of his words,
Digest
His own guts
Like a fasting
Monk,
Keep
A vow
Of silence
Made to a severe
Mother or father
In younger days,

Then vomit
Them out,
Gagging in
Peristaltic rhythm
The error of his,
And others' ways,
Or the beauty
He saw
But could not
Make stay,

Stepped on
His own words
Until he broke
Their shells,
And suddenly
They swarmed up
Like restless
Larvae from a well.
Or startled
Nesting birds.

Perhaps my father
Was a poet
After all,
His bronze head
Rests,
In my memory,
On a pillar
In a stately hall.

■ NATIVE CHILD OF LIGHT

The broad brim
Of Father's
Forties hat
Cast a slanted shadow
Across his refugee eyes,

Eyes to me
Like the sun
Covered by cloud,
I could not seem
To make my father proud.

Escaping them,
I contrived
A world of light,
A child alone
Under the Midwestern sky,

When on my own
The sun did shine,
My father's shadow
Could not reason
Or rhyme

The way a bird could,
Or define a butterfly,
As did I,
As a native child
Of light.

◨ SERPENT FATHER

I have killed you a thousand times,
But you have killed me a million.
Great snake father, serpent king,
Father of all that is royal,

And evil, all such snakes are killers,
Burrowing, blind, legless lizards.
Great fertile father, with organs of
Generation at each end,
In graceful combat-mating dance,

You who ate my world
And spit it out again,
Ate an egg called the moon,
A serpent swallowing a star,

You would do battle with the sun,
But I would warn him of your
Fang and venom, your feats
Of swallowing, your forked tongue.

Like you, I will never shut my eyes
Or blink, you, who leave your young
To die at birth, cold-blooded,
Squeezing the breath from a bird,

Blindly seeing all as one large
Threatening thing. Father, sacred viper,
I, your snake son, long hypnotized
By your eternal, staring eye,

I, who have outgrown my skin,
With new scales beginning again,
A rainbow serpent—venom curing venom
Only—will bite your head off.
See you in the cemetery!

⚎ SOMETHING TALL AND GERMAN

Feeling again today
As though something
Tall and German,
Like a great pine tree,
Were towering
Father-like
Above me,

Ready to command,
Or to judge
Or condemn me,
A work of music
Or poetry,

Ready to fall
From a sharp gash,
Slashing its way down,
Slithering
Through the forest
Like a felling
Of pine needles,

Hissing split wood,
Sinking its
Pointed summit fang
Into my low heart.
A work waiting to start.

THE NEED FOR MEMORY

■ THE PERFECT PRUSSIAN GENTLEMAN

Adolph Eichmann's
Ghost
Struts across
The T.V. screen
In another
Historical
Re-creation.

He points
His brain-bashing
Tea cup at me,
Threatening
With bull-dozer
Shoulders
Of his uniform-suit,
Bullet-buttons
Blazing,
Slender,
Cannon-collared neck
Hissing politely
At the lip,
Adam's apple
Ready to rip,

Lights flashing
From round,
Fascist glasses
Signaling attack,
Thin metal frames,
Fangs in front,
Talons in back,
He walks,
The perfect

Prussian gentleman,
His dainty shoes
Tank-treading
The carpet
To where I stand,
Steel and concrete
Bunker body
Holds out
A barbed wire hand.

◪ CHILDREN OF THE SUN

Children,
Thrown live
Into ovens,
Young birds,
Hurled against
Burning air,
Flying
Through flues,
Caught
In updrafts
Of searing wind,
Seared singing
Everywhere.
Incinerated
Nursery rhymes,
Cindered
Lullabies,
Fluted throats
Unsheathed
From seed,
Slender reeds,
Parched ancient
In an instant.

▦ HOLOGRAM
A DREAM

As in a hologram,
The chorus
Of the dead
Stands side by side
In one endless line,
Their cadaverous heads
All look
In one direction,
Off-stage
To the right,
They move as one
Toward the light.

As in a hologram,
Light
Is their resurrection,
As in the history
Of man,
Since he first sought
The cave's
Protection,
And saw the paintings
On his walls
Flicker
In the fire's
Endless reflection,
Dreaming of
An eternal caravan,
From the animal
To his own
Perfection.

◪ THE BIG WAR

The big war
Is not over yet,
Jet fighters still
Stitch the air space,
More modern,
More silent
Sewing machines,
Making more
Lethal lace.

The cows still look up
From their fields,
At a dark buzzing
Not made by flies,
The antennae
Of snails
Still scan
The dangerous skies.

■ THE ROOT OF HUMAN NEED

Even a tree
Survives
In us.
Even a tree
Cut down
Reminds us
That we
Loved it
Once.

Even a tree
Cut up
In pieces
Surprises,
With its
Mammoth
Elephant limbs
Of all sizes.

Even a tree
Survives
In memory,
Through
The root
Of human need.

■ ICE TREES

Once
Every so
Many years
The ice rain,
Frozen on the trees,
Sprayed and lacquered
In a quick freeze,
Coats
The blackened skeletons,
Their green flesh
Winter-ripped,

Yet suddenly
They erupt,
Glazed
As if by
Ice grapes
Hanging glistening
From overnight
Ripe vines,
Millions
Of glittering twigs,
Chandeliers clicking
In cold Spring wind,
Treetop candelabras
Waving flame.

Winter trees,
You seemed to have died
Yet now ignite,
Soon to bloom,
Roots fed by your own
Ice tears,
Cold, and clear,
And fine.

▥ THE PHOTOGRAPHER'S WALTZ

Seen at a wedding,
Dancing with his camera,
As bride and groom
Ride on heavy chairs
Around the room,
The photographer makes
Of his job of remembering,
A most graceful dance,
Assumes an erect posture
In his tuxedo,
Back arched like a penguin,
One hand holds the camera
To his handsome face,
The other downward,
Fingers glued together,
Like a fish's fin at his side,

The photographer
Moves to the music
As though he has
No need to hide,
He is part of
The dance of the lovers,
And his gliding
Helps them to glide.

Imagine him
Gliding through Europe,
His dance floor
The vast countryside,
The lovers are
All his people,
And in his dream,
Not one of them has died.

◼ NEO-NAZI

You are not new,
But old,
As old as the hills—
The bold killer,
An ancient snake
In a new garden,
Old Satan again,
Pleading to lie
And be pardoned.

It is hard
To be a man,
So you would kill
All the men
Of a small,
But powerful clan.

I know your plan.
You think
By killing them
You can take
Their power,
You think you can
Get the bouquet,
By killing
The flower.

◪ ANTI-SEMITE

Living on
An invisible
Equator
Circling
The globe
Dead center,

Pygmies
Of the planet
Tower
Next to these
Collapsible
Paper dragons,

These hate-boys
Schooled in rage,
Animals
Backed
Into a corner,

These lads
And ladies,
Backed into
The smallest
Corner on earth—
The narrow mind—

Screaming
Like dinosaurs
That they are going
To rule the world
As they fall
Into the slime,

Yes, those
Big muscles
Do make
Big fossils

As down they go,
Greedily,
Into the
Well-deserved dirt,

Their heavy brows
Furrowing
Fools gold
Into their vacant
Brain pans
And hollow
Hearts.

▚ NATURAL HISTORY MUSEUM

Here the reptiles
And lizards
Face one another,
Caught in a spell
Of marble halls,

They glare
At each other
Over eons of age,
Each filled
With an unnameable rage,
Each defending that place
On which their bodies
Are placed,
Each glaring the way
They happen to face.

Little difference
It makes,
Whether slinking skeleton
Of snake,
Or crawling lizard,
Or crouching ape,
Or striding man—
Their territory
Is their only clan.

◼ AIRPLANE CRASH

Each time
A giant wing
Bursts into fire,

Each time an engine
Falls off
Light as a feather
At high speed
And flies
Into its own eye,

Each time
A broken-winged body
Hits the ground,
Bursting into flame
And hot cry,

We see what it means
To fly too high.

◼ REFUGEE SONG

To parachute—
To fall nearby—
We are falling
All around,
Into every land,
From every sky,

Jumping
To safety
Or freedom,
Like flying
Squirrels,
But human,

Like babies
Dropping,
Arching
Silken wings,

Hanging
By harp-strings,
As we fall
In the wind,
We sing.

PART II

Family Reflections

PORTRAITS

◼ JEWISH AUSTRIAN AMERICAN

Like a needle in
A mother's porcelain breast,
A fish poisoned by its own,
To be both Jew and Austrian,

And then to be American,
The son of refugees,
Thrown off course
In an unfamiliar sea,
Stranded on beautiful
But foreign shore,

Fled from the gray Danube,
To the leafy Mississippi.

DICKERSON'S GROCERY STORE
(Catlin, Illinois)

We would walk together, my brother and I,
(Too small to ride bikes or go alone,)
The three blocks from our house
To Dickerson's,
The only grocery store in town,
A block from the only cafe.

Dickerson's, with the big
Plate glass window out front,
Letting most of the light there was
Into that dim canyon of cans.

Dickerson's, to us,
The biggest room around,
Except for the church and high school,
Bigger than the post office next door,
Or Charlie Gardner's soda parlor
Across the street, or Lonnie Hamm's
Barber shop with the one, high chair,
In the room built on the front of his house.
Not bigger, I remember now, than the bank,
But we may have been there only once.

Whereas Dickerson's was
The pantry of our home.
Any morning or afternoon,
Mother might send us there
For a can of Campbell's soup,
Or some good yellow American cheese,
That Mr. Hirschel Dickerson himself
Would pull from beside a gigantic
Red tube of balony
And cut slices miraculously thin,
With the whirling silver wheel-knife
That made us pull in our fingers.

Where Hirschel got all that food
We never thought to want to know,
But trudged with our fine, brown, smooth
Paper bag home through the sun or snow,
Doing the slow two-step dance
All children blessed with two feet do,
In time to the simple tin-can rhythm
Of their hearts' double-ended roll.

Our parade of two proudly passed
The reviewing stand,
Perhaps of a uniformed red cardinal
On a branch, festooned with
Orange berry pom poms,
In the white bunting snow.

▜ A BROTHER LIVING OUT HISTORY

Tense, an over-strung bow,
Threatening to smash
The arrow,
Crush its feathers
And sink a splintered beak
Into its own sweet heart,

A self-poisoned dart,
A human missile
Doomed from the start,
Living out history,
You cannot play,
But play your part.

▉ FOR A BROTHER, ON HIS WAY

You are still on your way
To America, my brother,

You still forge ahead,
Married a second time
In a white frame, Illinois
Country Unitarian church,
The sun spiraling off the spire

As the cobblestones of Amsterdam
Must have spiraled
Like the brightest sun,
The day our parents arrived
From Vienna on the run,
Their shared
Childhood left behind,
But ready to sail
On the Holland America Line.

Brother, with your Swedish-American
Lace bride, grasp the bell rope,
Ring the church bell,
Not of churches in those old streets
But this new Philadelphia freedom bell,
May you come to a land as free as we
When we were young twin pine cones
On a tree that was always green,
We fell into the good earth of Illinois,
And stayed a spell.

Brother, my first, best friend, my twin,
I am always with you, as you trudge
Along the white ocean shoals
Of drifted snow towards America,
Towards your warmest home,
I am with you as you grow up
In a tree house nest of boards,

In yellow cowboy birthday hat,
In constant costumes and then uniforms,

And now a doctor, with snake
Wound around your staff,
Determined you always were,
Never willingly to do harm,

My brother, as you approach America,
Bless you on your way.

▓ STAMP COLLECTING
(for a daughter)

Her hand hovers
Over the stamps.
They were my mother's,
Father's, mine.
She is twelve,

Piles them
On her white carpet,
Fluttering mounds
Of history,
Countries now forgotten,
Estonia, Austro-Hungary,
Names stamped on geography
And later removed,
Easily as her hand
Slips the stamps
Off with water.
Nations use blood.

Heroes, heroines
Of every costume,
Some that later
Turned villain.
Here an inflation stamp,
Ten million Marks.
There a young Hitler,
With fresh haircut,
Looking calm.
Now a post-war German stamp,
A voting booth.
And then the new ones,
The state of Israel.

The countries,
And their stamps—
Truly paradise

For a child.
Imagined by children,
The currencies, the flags.

They were our mothers',
Fathers', ours.
We have collected them
Since the world began,
And must find a place
For them all,
Before they are scattered
By a great wind—
Before we come of age.

⬛ MENOPAUSE

You have shrunk
To a young girl again,
My wife,
With no more blood
Or strife,
Just when our daughter
Is grown a woman,
Swelling with
The blood and flesh
Of life.

For you
The months pause,
The moon
Will no longer
Wax and wane
In your womb,
Be your boon
Or bane.

Now the hot dry sun
Flashes in the canyon,
Where once
The flash floods ran,
Through time and tons
Of pelvic stone,

The earth
And the man
Were young,
When you
With him
Spawned a son.

Now a girl again,
Dreaming
Of all the children

You might have borne,
From the plenty
Of your spiral horn,

In this,
God's dollhouse of the stars,
You play your new
Galactic mother's part.

⌘ THE OCEAN OF THE HUMAN DOMAIN

Like fireworks
In the night,
Our generations
Fly up
And disappear.

See
The fiery rose,
And there,
The midnight sunflower
Made of wandering
Fire flies.

Green stems of flame
Push through
The earth of night
Spelling out,
In cursive starlight,
Our family names.

Swimming forward
In slow celestial time,
As fish through
Underwater trees,
We glide through
Our family fates,

Our larger species
And smaller name,
Star sent and guided,
Often against our will
And without respite,
Into the ocean
Of the human domain.

PHOTOGRAPHS

◪ FLICKER BOOK

Onkel Leopold
Still sits
In the garden
In Vienna,
In this photo,
As he must have
When the man
And woman
Who were to be
My parents,
Looking grim,

Came to him
To ask
Whom he knew
In America
To sign an affidavit
That would let them in.

Onkel Leopold flicks
Through his address book,
The flame
Of my unborn life
Flickers dim
For that moment,
Until he finds them,
The Kaufman cousins
In Cleveland—

Oh, the flicker books
We knew as children,
Letting still pages
Go flying
Through the air,
Making there
Moving-pictures,
What were once
Disjointed parts

Would grow whole
And come alive,

As what flickers,
Frowning
In the dark,
May reveal
The smile
Of starlight.

▦ GOD'S GLOVE

"Hand shoes,"
The German word
For gloves,
These gloves were indeed
Shoes for my parents,
They carried
Mother and Father
To America,
Paupered by Hitler,

Mother sewed them
While Father took
His medical degree again.
My daughter wants them.
She says:
"I'll wear them to my prom."
Yes, these gloves
Were meant for promenades,

Silken chamois
And floral lace,
White kid
Buttoned at the wrist,
Or elbow-length leather
Soft as a hand-kiss,
Garments of my parents'
Own younger days—

Sweet-scented,
Leather flower petals,
Pink Lady's Slipper,
Lilac, Violet,
Dust Rose,
God's Glove.

A WAVE OF THE HANDS OF THE SEA

Grandfather William's
Pocket watch
Is stopped
At one twenty-seven
Vienna time,
Nineteen thirty-nine.

Some seeds
And some songs
Die,
But the seeding
And the singing go on.

I wind
Grandfather William's
Watch,
Miraculously
It ticks again,
Like seeds
From dry pods
Ticking
In the wind,

Like songs
Of children,
Trailing off
And trailing on,
While building temples
On the seashore
Of songs and sand,

As a wave
Of the hands
Of the sea
Tells the time
To begin again.

■ PICTURE BOOKS

Where did they come from,
These Austrian picture books
Mother read to us
As American children?
Brought from Vienna perhaps,
Though strange things
To pack in a steamer trunk
When fleeing danger.

And why read them
To us,
About to grow up
In America.
For nostalgia?
Or that we would learn
The language
Of our parents' birth?

Perhaps Mother
Could not bear
To understand,
The country's hand
Which had rocked
Her own cradle
Was a murderous hand.

The same hand,
With foot-long claws,
I see in this book,
"Shock-headed Peter,"
Where the boy who
Did not perfectly clean
His fingernails or hair,
Terribly suffers,

Or the hand of Klaus,
Who lost his shoe,
And to pay for the mistake

Had to do forced labor,
Or Konrad,
Whose poor prohibited
Sucked thumb
Was bloodily cut off—

Like the lives
Of Jewish children.

◪ FATHER

"Don't smile,"
Photographers
Must have said.
At the time
When this early photo
Was made,
That was the style
In those days,
Serious, dignified,
Not light and gay.
You were a good boy, Father,
For the times in Vienna,
You posed the right way.

I find you
In this photograph
In nineteen fifteen,
At the age of six,
Dressed by a common
Photographer's trick
In the costume of
An Austrian military prince.

Toy sword at your side,
Double-breasted jacket,
High-collared, with a star,
Buttoned, knee-high spats,
Still innocent,
Yet preparing,
Are you aware
That your country
Is at war?

They always said
Of your family
That they only laughed
On the back stairs,
Anyhow, a serious lot—

Yet now here you are,
In another picture,
A smiling young man,
With a soft neck tie,
And your pet terrier.

◫ MOTHER

You always told me
You were never beautiful,
But you were wrong.
More than just the beauty
Of youth in song,
Or the adoring duty
Of every mother's son,

I can see
From these old photographs,
Your chubby baby portrait
Dangling in a locket
From your lamb chop
Moustached grandfather's
Fobbed watch chain,
You were a dark-haired,
Dark-eyed little queen.

At two,
You wore lace epaulettes
On your fat shoulders.
At sixteen,
You were slim,
A school girl
In sailor's pinafore,
White-collared.

At twenty,
You wore pearls.
No longer a young girl,
You were moonlight
In a flowered dress,
Yes, a shining sight.

In your twenties,
White flapper hat
Pulled down around
Your desert-night

Black eyes,
In your thirties,
Your Viennese brooch
Was a crown.

Mother,
In full flower —
I see you now.

▓ SMILING

Father,
Your baby smile
Took a while
To appear,
I find it here,
In photographs
Of nineteen twenty-nine,
On your own
For the first time
In your twentieth year.

You and your
Medical classmates
Look happy
In your white coats,
You had one friend
Who was funny,
Here you smile,
With your arm
On his shoulder,
Here he strikes
A ballet pose
With pointed toe.

You and Mother
Were going steady,
A constant,
Smiling number,
Easy and close,
On the beach,
The tennis court,
In local resorts
Around Vienna,
You were students,
You were informal,
You were very
Much in love,
Life was normal.

BIRTH YEAR: CHICAGO
(After Carl Sandburg)

Chicago was born
In Spring,
When prehistoric
Star-serpents
Wrapped
Among black
Coral trees.
Fish with
Butterfly-wings
And lizard-spines
Swam, flew,
And crawled.
Defenseless plants
Made thorns
To ward off
Herbivores.
Flowers learned
To multiply,
And so
Outlived
The dinosaurs.

I was born
Near Chicago
In Spring,
Born as all plants,
Trees and flowers
That have ever been,
As all animals
Fish and birds
That ever lived
Were born,
All eggs hatched
Of all insects.

I was taken out
For a first walk

In Spring,
As all babies
Are carried out.
All young women, men
And old people
Come out in Spring.
I heard the animals
And birds call out,
The babies,
Young men and women.
All old people sing
In Spring.

I was born
And am still alive,
They sing.
I am still alive,
Sings every plant
And animal,
Every fish and bird,
I was born,
Sings every baby,
Woman, man,
Every old person,
And I am still alive.
Every tree,
Flower, insect,
Every song
And story says,
I am still alive.

The wind says,
I was born
And am still alive,
The water, the rocks,
The sun, still alive,
The planets,
The galaxies,
Born and still alive.

⌗ OUR PARENTS' WALTZ

It is
The last time
I can
Remember them
Waltzing together,
At the Danville,
Illinois
Viennese Ball,
In the auditorium
Of the Veteran's
Hospital.

My father,
Tall in his tuxedo,
In his sixties,
Few years to go.
My mother,
I cannot remember
What she wore,
But for me
She wears a gown
Of teardrop pearls.

I watch them
From the bleachers,
Among the Illinois
Waltz-walkers,
Blackwhite
They whirl.

▟ HEAVEN HELMET
(for a statue unveiling, Catlin, Illinois)

This black candle
Throws a bronze flame,
My father,
Much mourned—
Is now to be
A little famed.

But wake up
Any number of the dead
Who have had
Bronze busts
Made of them
And they will say:
"What's all the fuss?
I did nothing
To deserve this."

Once a poet,
Blinded
For a while
By a bronze
Life-mask,
Said:
"That's when I learned
All I want to know
Of human pride,
The bronze laurel
Almost stole
Away my eyes."

So, half way between
Stone age and bronze—
Deeds before they are begun,
And after they are done—
Falls the age of iron,
The time of doing deeds
And getting small reward,

For any child who mourns
A parent knows,
That bronze is made
For statues or for bells,
And this is just my father
With his heaven helmet on.

PART III

Return Visits

TO GERMANY AND AUSTRIA

▟ LUFTHANSA, LEAGUE OF THE AIR

I watch the dawn come up
Like a white cup-lip
Around the black tea of ocean,
Drink in the uncreated night,
Wait for the sun to shine
Again for the first time,
The night's black dawn bouquet,
Petals on a white, tufted
Tablecloth of cloud mist spray.

My fourteenth flight to Germany
In fourteen years,
Deep in the silver belly
Of a Lufthansa whale,
Like Jonah,
Having first been afraid
To sail to Nineveh where,
The Jews are still blamed
For every gale,
Thrown overboard
To feed the fish of fear.

Forty-nine years old,
Forty-nine years since
The end of the war,
A living calendar
Created by the war,
Trailing back and forth
Between America and Europe,
Not sure
What I keep looking for.

▣ TANTE ELSA

Dance, Tante Elsa,
Dance the Polonaise,
In your nightgown,
Gown of night,
Jewish German girl
Of seventy-eight,

Let others sit
In the Einstein Cafe,
You were not born
For coffeehouse haze,
Rawboned as an ox,
Content, you graze,

Though Onkel Fritz,
Your friend and lover,
Sleeps under
The grass of the grave,
Though all the doors
Of a country of ice
Had been smashed
In a single night,
And every crystal vase,

You would still
Walk the heather,
Red with the heart's
Bud-blaze,
And dance away the night
As you wait for the world
To grow wild enough,
To grow wise.

⊞ SLOW PSALM IN GERMANY

Is this glistening snail
In this black forest
To blame?
Is it,
After so many gentle rains,
Also to bear the shame?

Still listening
As it must have,
As Goethe did
When he was just fourteen,
To Mozart, a boy of seven,
Playing in the wind.
As ancient sea snails
Must have heard the world
When this was just
A nation of birds.

Will these tadpoles
In this stream
Be forced to hear again,
Not Mozart's instrument,
The well-tempered breeze,
But the sad scream
Of wind on metal fin,
Born to wring the world
Back to stone again?

Back to silent melody
Of crystal teeth
Under solar sea,
Humming for a million years,
Psalms slow to grow as
Stoney snails
Climbing up
Green coral trees.

▦ MOZART IN AUSCHWITZ

It is dawn.
The rain has written music
All night
On the tin roof.
Come here
To this crack of window.
See the rose-blue sky
Behind the pines.
Listen to the birds
Play their flutes.

I am here
In Auschwitz
Accused of degeneracy,
Because I cannot make a living.
I write music all night long
Until I faint in the morning.
I am afraid I will never finish
My hymn to the country
I believed in.

My hymn,
The first German opera,
Magic Flute, begun
After I moved with my wife
Onto the Street of The Jews
In Vienna,
Because we were poor too.

I am a man-child,
Wrote music since I was three,
And now that I am twenty-three,
Still cannot believe
That my country
Would be here,
Digging
Its own grave
In these fields.

▓ HITLER RADIO

It invades my head
Like a terrible song,
Playing scratchily
Along the grooves
Of some trail
Of tragic passion
And madness,

The sight of this old,
German radio,
From a sidewalk
In small, modern, Mulheim,
Through the window
Of a music store,
In a trendy
Dummy display.

"Das ist ein Hitler Radio,"
Tante Elsa says in lowered tone,
Of this simple box of wood
And cloth-covered microphone,
Faded, torn,
Nothing more,
Except the plastic ivory
Of the yellow dial,
A band as thin as flat bone,

With magic names carved in it:
London, Berlin, Paris, Rome,
Istanbul, Cairo, Tokyo,
And, not visible, Auschwitz,
Bergen-Belsen, Buchenwald, Dachau,
Theresienstadt, Treblinka, Chelmno.

▦ BAD BOY, ADOLF

You started
Your speeches out
Soft and low,
The way your mother,
Weak and gentle,
Spoke to you,
Then built
To a screaming
Crescendo,
The way your weak
And brutal father
Used to do.

Your speeches,
A witches brew
Of old fashioned
Values,
Honor, obedience,
And all
For the Fatherland,
The land became
A father to you,
But you felt yourself
The victim once again,
This time
Of a God-fathered
People,
The Jews.

You were the son
Of bad parents,
And a bad boy,
Adolf,
A genius of chaos,
A negative messiah,
Fifty million
People's grave.

ON KURT TUCHOLSKY'S 100th BIRTHDAY

Kurt Tucholsky,
You would have been
A hundred years old
Today,

Honored now in Germany
As you were then
Exiled and banned,
Your books burned
In the thirties.

Master
Of the German cabaret,
I might have seen you
On the stage,
I could have been
Your protégé—

Without your language
And your home,
Poison suicide
On a Swedish
Spring day —

A prisoner
Of your own escape.

⊞ THE PARACHUTIST

In Mauthausen
Concentration Camp,
He sees from high
On the cliff
What look like
Black ants,
Scaling the huge
Granite steps
Up from the quarry
With stone
On their backs.

The parachutist
Prefers it
To the gas shower
Or gallows.
Let his skin and
Teeth be there,
Not in
A coal-oven fire.
Let him fall
From here,
Not from standing
On a chair.

Remembering—
Once he fell asleep
On a dock
Of the Moon Sea,
The sea still,
The mountains high,
The trees green,
And as he fell asleep,
A pheasant's wings
Sheered open
Above him.

♜ THE SULZBURG CEMETERY

1.
As I walk through the cemetery gate-house,
I see the steps on the hill rise up steeply,
Seven at a time, level out, then rise again,
On each terrace, two candelabra-like trees,
And straight rows of graves, laid out
As if trellises for vineyards on a hill.
Here the only crop is moss.

Walking among the graves, I try to press
From the moss their secret stories—
Who were these people,
To bury each other on a hidden mountainside,
Inscribed in a sacred, foreign tongue,
So far from the village,
As though to build here
A city of their own.

2.
Another passing stranger asks of me:
"What is this place?" "A cemetery
Of the Jews," I say, "five hundred years old,
Unknown, and so left undisturbed."
I walk away, still among the graves,
Seeing snails—the clearest signs of life—
That on the hillside tend the vineyards of moss,
Climbing up the shifting sandstone of graves,
Like camels seen far off in a desert.

Perhaps they know
What journey brought these people here,
Carrying their belongings with them so slowly
Their packs must have seemed like tombs,
Rising mountain-like over their flesh.
To those without a home,
Everything higher than a head
Looks like a home.

3.
How quiet it is.
A peddler,
Five hundred years ago,
Walks from village to village,
Here in the Black Forest of Germany.
He buys and sells rags
Each season to live,
Like a snake sheds skins,

And is treated like a snake
By the savage farmers' dogs,
Who fear the unfamiliar familiarity
Of his slithering pace,
The way he seems to curl in circles,
As if to hide his face.

The dogs have snapped
At his rags before,
Like their masters,
Who see him also as a snake,
Human reptile from the Bible,
A freak of nature
They have dreamed in sleep,
Like the hideous stuffed animals
The farmers create,
A rabbit with beak of hawk, or horns of deer,
The Jew perhaps the cause of all their woe,
Because they know no other cause.

4.
Now the peddler's seed
Sits in the synagogue in town,
And hears a tap at the window.
He has a house, a wife, children,
And he is afraid.
He shakes, as the peddler shook,
Peasants and dogs

Have risen up to rule again,
Now with machines in their hands,
And once again they cry out for rags,
Clothes, bandages, and
Again they cry out against the Jew.
A tap at the window—
"All Jews to the railroad station!"

5.
Five hundred years have arranged
And rearranged these sandstone
Pieces on this board,
Playing a serious game
To see if they can win,
This once,
A prize away from time.

Here, a tree holds up
A stone from falling,
There, one has laid
A marker down to rest,
Tree and tomb grown together,
Leaning toward each other,
Lovers kissing in a silent place,
And in that place around the heart,
Where love and desire
Cannot be pulled apart,
I want something of what is here.

6.
From a pile of discarded rubble
In the cemetery,
A fragment of a gravestone
Flies to America
On a Lufthansa jet,
Wrapped in brown paper,
Sitting in a shopping bag
In the garment bin

At the back of the plane,
Disguised as a piece of clothing,
Another kind of rag,
Traveling away
From the Sulzburg cemetery
At nearly the speed of sound.

TWO TRANSLATIONS

▦ I AM SO MUCH AT HOME AND
AM ALREADY NO LONGER HERE
(*Theodor Kramer, Vienna, 1939*)

I am so much at home, and am already no longer here,
What writings that I have, I always carry near;
The corners are dust filled, the clothes are wearing fine,
The bed, in which I sleep, is already no longer mine.

Where I will go, still today I do not know,
Only, like a duty, I know that I must go.
I think about it, I recite it to myself;
It refuses to become clear, it will not penetrate my ear.

Seeking out acquaintances, seldom enters my head,
It can never be a beginning, only an end.
The word, that wanted to greet, is today no longer there,
I seem to myself for weeks, as though hanging in the air.

From what once was, I am long divided by a tear;
That all is unsure, is all that is sure.
Even the mouse has its hole; if they don't nest, starlings
Migrate...only Man goes on existing toward nothing.

Author's translation from Kramer's *Verbannt Aus Osterreich,*
(Banned From Austria) Austrian P.E.N.,
London, 1943.

WHO IS RINGING OUTSIDE THE DOOR
(*Theodor Kramer, Vienna, 1939*)

Who is ringing outside the door,
When it is barely dawn?
I'll go, my darling. It's just the boy
Who's set some fresh rolls down.

Who is ringing outside the door?
Just stay, I'm on my way, my child.
It was a man; he asked our neighbor
Who we are.

Who is ringing outside the door?
Fill, my darling, your bath tub full.
The mail was here, but not the letter
I was waiting for.

Who is ringing outside the door?
Go air out the beds.
It was the janitor:
He said on the first we are terminated.

Who is ringing outside the door?
The fuchsia bloom so near.
Pack, dearest, for me my wash kit
And don't cry: they are here.

Author's translation from Kramer's *Verbannt Aus
Osterreich (Banned From Austria)*, Austrian P.E.N.,
London, 1943.

SIMON WIESENTHAL

▚ SIMON WIESENTHAL:
MEMORY OF AN INTERVIEW
(*Vienna, 1985*)

There are not words in any language
To express what happened,
Because words are the product of culture,
And what happened was a return to the beast.
No one would believe it anyway,
That was the Nazi's plan;
They thought: "No one will believe it,"
And they were right. I myself
Went through the camps,
Saw the beatings and the killings,
But even then I did not believe in the ovens.
Words cannot capture what happened,
Because we were reduced by hunger
To caring about nothing—only food.
I was, at the end, imprisoned at Mauthausen;
We were given 200 calories a day;
We had no work to do;
We lay on boards all day long
On death row. Even to think was exhausting,
And I remember with me in the cell
Were three French people—not Jewish—
And one spoke of a meal he had once eaten
At the Ritz Hotel in Paris,
And another said he had tasted
A dish from the meal made another way.
A third man, on the top board,
Lifted his hand, and said, "with Parmesan,"
Dropped his hand, and died.
You see, this is why words don't work;
If you told that to someone, they would laugh.

All the words in the world would not be sufficient
To describe one day in the camps.
I read Solzhenitsyn's book, *One Day in the Life,*
And yet it does not capture what happened.

Perhaps poetry could, because poems say
In a single word more than a book.
I knew Yiddish poets, they were my friends,
But they are dead, the Yiddish language is dead,
There was no poetry in the camps,
And now my one friend who is a poet
Keeps silent.

But for you it is better to write than not,
Words are information,
And information makes one safer.
That was our problem, we Jews,
We did not have enough information,
We believed in European civilization;
We did not know it was so thin,
As thin as the skin on your hand.
That is what I resent most,
That they damaged my sense of human dignity;
I resent that most of all.
Not everyone reacted this way,
But I was hurt by it.
There was a Nazi whom I testified against
At the trials—not that he was the worst,
He was part of the whole machine,
A murderer, but not a sadist—
And he said when he saw me:
"I recognize Wiesenthal,
He always stood upright."
It bothered the Nazis,
That I was tall, and I always stood
With my head up,
So I got beaten more than the others.

Our whole generation has been destroyed by it,
Even those who lived;
We are not normal;
I am not normal;
It is not normal to spend
One's whole life remembering—

Or like some, forgetting—
Or like others, seeking honor,
Saying, "I lived through it,
Only I know."

The people with the worst consciences
In the world are Jews.
They feel, "I could have done something,
I should have said something."
Now they are writing to me—
When I no longer need them—
A millionaire from Maryland called me
To ask if I would find the killer of his father.
I said: "Do you have documentation?"
He replied: "My brother and I witnessed it."
I said: "Where have you been for 20 years?"
And he began to cry.

The best film I have seen on those times
Is *In the Garden of the Finzi-Continis;*
There was shown what happened to a family
Without a single shot being fired.
Atrocity is boring, you know,
One cannot sit and watch it.
For those who lived it,
Documentary shows too little,
For those who didn't,
It is too much, they turn off the T.V.
I spent hours editing footage
Out of a film we made called *Genocide,*
Cutting out bearded faces so people today
Would not think Jews primitive tribesman,
Making it short, so people would listen.

Sometimes someone comes along
Who can express, in a letter,
In a few words,
What others could never express.

I knew such a man,
The most brilliant I ever met—
It was Robert Kennedy.
I once asked him for an article
For a book I wrote opposing
The statute of limitations—
200 professors sent long articles—
But Kennedy sent a telegram:
MORAL DUTIES HAVE NO LIMITS.
Five words.

We are the last ones left.
I am seventy-six;
After us there is only history;
It will not be what happened,
But only resemble what happened.
That's all I can say.
Please send the poems you wrote about me
Here to the center, we will put them in the archives—
Perhaps I will send them to my grandchildren.

PART IV

Historical Reflections

MODERN PORTRAITS

◪ HERZL IN BASEL

In the well known
Photograph,
Theodor Herzl
Stands
On a bridge,
In 1897,
Overlooking
The river
In Basel,
Switzerland.

Incomprehensibly
Elegant,
Dark, tall,
Erect and alone,
He has crossed
The Rubicon
And can never
Return,

Like a bearded
Messenger
In savage,
Ancient Greece,
Soon to die
For bearing news
No one wishes
To receive,

That Jews in Germany
Will never be loved
As Germans,
But always be hated
As Jews,
And worse,
That for Europe
And the world,
The same is true.

Herzl stands
On the bridge,
His eyes
In the old
Photograph
Seem to turn
From side
To side,

Like the two
Great fiery wheels
Burning
In the prophet
Elijah's eyes,
When, angel-like,
His chariot
Began to rise.

The flames of Europe
Burn in
One of Herzl's eyes,
And in the other,
The flames
Of Palestine.

And in
The old picture,
Between the two eyes,
On the brow gazing
Across the river,
Blazes the flame
Of the angel's sword
Guarding the gate
To paradise.

◼ PAPER ROSE
(for Hannah Senesh, poet,
executed in 1944)

Hannah,
The paper rose
You made
For your mother
In prison
Still blows,

Hannah,
The paper rose
You fashioned
For your mother's
Birthday
When you were
Both in prison
In Budapest
Still blows,

Hannah,
The paper rose
You sent
Your mother,
Who taught you
To be brave
Enough
To parachute
Back to Hungary
From Palestine
To help save
Your people
Still blows,

Hannah,
The rose
Of red blood
You spilled
On the snow,

Refusing
The blindfold
At the wall
In Budapest,
Still blows

Across
The sandstone
Of Jerusalem,
Hannah,
The paper rose
You made,
Hannah,
The blood red rose.

▥ FOR NELLY SACHS, POET

Childless Nelly,
Mother of all
Poet-moths
Drawn back
To Europe's
Flame,

Escaped
In 1940
From Berlin
To Stockholm,

You must
Have walked
Along the water
As if by
Imaginary canals
On
The desolate moon,

Living with
Your mother
In a few
Poor rooms—

She, the old
Frau Sachs,
Sat at the window,
While you, Nelly,
Mourned
The millions
Of mothers,

Turning your
Written scrolls,
Year in and out,
From death

Back to birth,
In your
Cradle-tomb,

Nelly,
Rocking by the sea,
With only
Falling leaves and
Washing seashells
For armor,

You took up arms
Against death's
Most recent monarchy,
And won,
Single-handedly.

◨ SOMEWHERE NEARER JERUSALEM
(for Paul Celan, poet, suicide, 1970,
and Anselm Kiefer, painter)

As Paul Celan
Sommersaults
And cartwheels
Off a bridge
In Paris,
Into the Seine,

The lines
From his poems
Spinning
In his head
Are caught
And juggled
By a
German painter,

Along with
Mud
On giant
Canvas,
Fields
Of dirty
Flaxen hair,
German
Peasant life
So far
From Paris,

Tar-covered
Books,
Rusted
Ankle-traps,
Windless
Furnace rooms

Scrawled
With the names
Of culture,
Horse troughs
Full of blood—

Verses
From the dead
Celan,
Dashed
Across the canvas,
Jewish poet and
Christian painter
Leapfrogging
Through the mud,

A single match flame
Falling into the Seine,
And emerging
Somewhere
Nearer Jerusalem.

﷽ THROUGH HIS OWN STONE'S CRACK
(for Primo Levi, poet, suicide, 1987)

They keep falling,
Crematorium dust
Keeps falling,
Whether loud
Bone ash
Rattling
In a box,
Or quietly
Sifting
Comet splash,

The latest
Heard of today,
Primo Levi
In Italy,
Running
Full speed,
Jumping from
His own balcony,
Fell four flights
Down his own
Marble stairwell,

Escaped—
Through his own
Stone's crack.

ANCIENT PORTRAITS

ᛘ KING DAVID IN DACHAU

King David still broods
Through the terrible
Small streets,
He searches
For the children
Of Israel,
Through piles
Of shoes
Light as snowflakes
In the mounds of snow,
Deserted children's coats,
Their bent arms,
Duck wings, broken.

Tiny felt caps,
Hollow turtle shells,
Empty mittens, stranded fish
With one, lifeless thumb-fin
Pointing in the air.

Where, where are they,
Youngest of God's children,
Most strictly ruled,
Most vulnerable to His rod?

David finds a cloth doll
Filled with corn husks,
A leather ball and wooden hoop,
A drawing of a fence, a tree, the sun,
A poem about death, freedom, love—
And in the sky, a silver ball
Called "Moon,"
And a pet-dove's eye
Called " Evening Star."

■ HITLER TO BATHSHEBA

"It was you
Who began the temple
I tried to destroy,
From you came
Solomon the builder,
Conceived with David the king,
That volcano roaring down
Into the ocean of your bath,
From your union cooled
The temple stone
I almost crushed to dust."

Pointing her gold hairbrush
At him, she laughs:

"It was you
Who thought love dies,
Deceived by a volcano
Long asleep before your eyes.
But true love always runs
Cool to molten again,
And rebuilds its temple
From a dust
Much finer than sand."

▓ HOLOCAUST PSALM

Holocaust,
Tree of Evil,
Gnarled beyond
Our knowing,
Or so
You would
Have us know,

Thousand knotted,
Growths upon
The growing,
Grown beyond
Our knowing
Of how
Things grow,

Thicker than faith
Sometimes is,
Tall as
Our travail,
And black as tar,

Holocaust of Heaven,
You would shut
The sun out,
And blot out
All of the stars.

▦ THE SWORD

Wedged deepest
In the brain,
Is the sword
Of pain,

Of life
And death,
Of breath
And no breath.

The bud dies
The blossom is born,
The blossom dies
The leaf is born,

After the leaf
The branch is born,
After the branch
The trunk is born,

The trunk dies
The worm is born,
Life and death
Turn and turn.

Life is nursed
By death,
Sung to
By her bitter breath,

Life on death's bosom
Rests until,
Life is weaned
At last,

To kill
Or create,

The sole two choices,
Our test,

To take hold of the sword
And to make,
Tall monuments to life—
Or to death.

■ WARRIOR

White blossom,
Young Knight,
Always believing
You are right,

That everyone
Is one to whom
Your song
Can be sung,

That you
Could never
Bring another
Doom.

Red leaf,
Red Knight,
Always believing
You must fight,

That everyone
Is one with whom
Your battle
Can be won,

That you can rage
And rampage
Without ever
Being wrong.

Green tree,
Green Knight,
Believing you àre
Not always right,

That everyone
Is one of whom

You must say, there
But for grace, go I,

That you
Must stand
With gnarled trunk,
But stand — upright.

◨ TRUE MAN

I am a member
Of
The killer-clan
Called Man.

I cannot remember
A time in time's
Span, when to kill
Was not my plan.

A man
Who will not kill
Is not a man, and
I know that I can.

I can burn
A village down to
Sand, or dirt, mud
Or stone land.

I can rape, murder
With my own hand,
And think
I am grand.

I am by heritage,
Man, descended
From
The weasel clan.

I am from the family
Of Lynx, Otter, Mink,
Ermine, Badger.

I am a tree Weasel,
A wound on wood,
A green-leaf
Cobra-hood.

I plan,
Some day,
Perhaps to become
A tree again.

◪ PEACE FIRE

A tree is a
Gigantic nation
To a blade
Of grass,

Even a tree
Cannot grow
In the shadow of
Another's path,

Everything
Must own
Its own place
On earth.

History seems to
Tell, man loves war,
And longs to kill
Or else be killed,

Bearded
Or female,
Always taking
To the field,

Claiming the one
Out there,
The enemy,
Will be revealed

To be the wolf
Hunting our sheep,
Wanting to come
Too near.

But we are each sheep
And wolf by turns,
We are near-by trees,
Peace-fires burning.

⌗ RACIST APOCALYPSE

Fighting
In the natural world
Is not inviting
To the animal,

The rabbit fights
The lynx
To stay alive,
Not because it thinks

Its enemy is bad,
The lamb
Must know the lion
From the ram

For safety,
Animals discriminate
To see their enemies,
Not from hate.

An animal
Is smarter than a man,
It can fight the one,
Without fighting the clan,

Man's heart races,
His brain does not keep pace,
He breeds weapons faster than
Images of the human face,

He first fought beasts of prey,
Now is a beast who preys,
And prays he is not feasting
On his final day.

Soon the lion, eagle, ox,
Beasts of the apocalypse,

Will come to cheer him,
Or to mock,

Riding in a chariot, like
A giant, uprooted tree, long buried
Waist high in the ground, racing up
Toward heaven, or racing down.

⌗ JERUSALEM OF BONE

When we rebuild
The heavenly city,
Let us rebuild
Jerusalem of bones,
Dig them up
From our graves
And lay them down
As entrance ways.

Take the skeletons
From our homes,
The swollen skulls
And rib-cages
Of hate,
And fashion
Windows
And gates.

Make our long bones
Towers,
The short ones
Meal
For flowers,
Make our marrow
Into mortar
For a city
Of heavenly stone.

Let us rebuild
Jerusalem of bones.

PART V

The Present

TANTE ELSA IN THE GARDEN
OF AMERICA

▜ BONE MEAL

Tante Elsa,
In your
First-class passenger
Lufthansa
Stockinged feet—
To keep your shoes
Out of the mud—

Wings on ankles,
You wade raw-boned
Through the blooms
And buds
Of the garden
You have made—

Littered with spades,
Pitchforks and hoes,
Peat moss,
Cow manure—

You sink new bushes
Into dirt as though
Bone meal were
All you knew
Of life on earth,
Bringing flowers
Out of bones,
Your only work.

GARTEN TRÄUMEREIEN
(Garden Dreams)

Elsa's garden has become
A small paradise
In a courtyard enclosure
On our patio, like those
Of my great grandsires on
Poor farms in Austro-Hungary,

Here,
She has planted flowers,
This harvest
Purely for the eyes,
Blue Danubes,
Aztec Golds,
As if to say
Whole civilizations arise
For no other reason
Than to praise—

That the rose may thrive—
To keep the soil moist,
Our prayer,
To keep from
Going dry,
As we pass
From young to old,
From first—
To last paradise.

TANTE ELSA IN THE GARDEN

Elsa knows the plants,
Their green
And flowered language
Speaks to her
Of sun and shade,
Of annual and perennial—
She, the perennial maid,
In a garden
That is always young.

She says:
"Flowers are like love,
Both must be gently won,
Flowers need soft beds,
They grow best
With kind words
And water
Warmed by the sun."

She says: " Your home
Can be a paradise,"
And now I see it
Through her eyes,
Trees and grass
And quiet sky,
And flowers in a vase,
Green and blue,
Red, and white,
Creation, fall,
And return to the light.

◫ PLANTING AS A DANCE

Tante Elsa has coaxed
Along with her
To our patio
The butterflies,
Not from Europe, no,
They were always here
In neighboring skies,
But now appear,

Drawn to the flowers
On which they feed,
To the fountain
Where they drink
And fold their wings,
As though freed
From flying
In the air,
They rest
Where water springs,

Enacting the law
Of planting
As a dance,
Floor of earth,
Music of seed,
Rhythm of rain,
Sway of wind,
New life,
New dance-steps,
Fresh costumes
Blossoming.

◰ WITCHING - WAND

The one
With the witching-wand
Walks the ground,
Green forked branch
In front,
Until it starts
To jump,
A demon snake
With forked tongue
In the wand-witcher's
Hands.

As though that
Were not enough,
Elsa tells me
Folk wisdom has it,
When a person cannot sleep,
It may be
Because water runs
Deep in a river
Under their bed,
A restless riverbed
Keeps them unrested,
Until they change rooms
To sleep.

Tante Elsa with her gift
Has shown how to find
The underground stream,
A healer who lays her hands
On trees,
A snake charmer
In the Garden
Of Eden.

▙ MOMENT IN THE GARDEN

There comes a moment
When life is at its highest,
Happy as you will ever be,
A moment containing
All the other moments
Of your life,
Past and future,
All you ever were
Or will be,

Contains them as a flower
Contains the seed it was
And the fruit it will become,
The seed of memory,
The fruit of prophesy.

When this moment comes,
Chances are
You will know it.
Your parents, children,
Mate, friends
Will be all around you,
Whatever makes up your life
Will be near.

You will be aware,
And perhaps a little sad,
Knowing that this
Is the happiest moment,
The fullest flowering
Of who you are,

Between the seeding
And the mowing,
You will know
Where you have been,
And you will know
Where you are going.

And in this moment
You will know
It has all been worthwhile,
Because your life has been
For the sake of this moment,
For the sake of this perfection.

You will be sun
And moon and stars,
And for this moment
In the garden,
You will thank God
By whatever name you know.

▓ PARADISE SONG

There is a love
That knows nothing
Of death,
There is a tree
That is a king
With a crowned head,

There is a fountain
Overflowing
With a rainbow
Of blossoms,
There is a stream
That is singing
The oldest of psalms.

There is a love
That knows nothing
Of death,
There is a tree
That is a queen
With a crowned head,

There is a fountain
Overflowing
With a rainbow
Of blossoms,
There is a stream
That is singing
The oldest of psalms.

There is a love
That knows nothing
Of death . . .

LADDERS

▉ SCALEWINGED

My tears climb
Down the ladders
Of my cheeks,
And in my mouth,
As words,
Scale up
To my brain again.

A child's
First ladder
Is a mother,
The child climbs her
Limb by limb,
Upwards
Toward the smile
That is heaven.

All children know
The world is made
Of ladders,
Green ones of grass,
White ones of snow,
Brown tree ladders—
All fathers—
And blue ladders
Of waves on water,

The ladder of
The sun's yellow,
And the moon's
Silver haze,
And every
Scalewinged seed,
Moth, butterfly
And bird—

Even the rainbow
In the stone,
Climbing up
From land
On light
Toward home.

⌗ THE LADDER OF MEMORY

Remember what you said
In the morning,
Remember the promises
You made
In your prayers
When you first awaked,

Remember that you made
Promises to God
And to yourself
When you were a child,
In the early morning
Of your life,
When you walked outside
When your heart was wild,
And you prophesied:

Some day I will climb
A ladder to the sky,
Some day I will wear a coat
Like a butterfly.
Some day I will grow
As tall as a tree,
Some day I will carry water
To the highest leaf.

Some day I will sink
My roots down in the earth,
And not the strongest wind
Will pull me from my berth.
Some day I will spread
My roots so wide,
That they will span the planet
And come out the other side.

Remember what you said
In the morning,
Remember the promises
You made
When you first awaked.

Remember you are always
Near the morning
Of your life.
Step onto
The ladder of memory,
And start to climb.

ABOUT THE AUTHOR

David Koenig was born on March 25, 1944, in Danville, Illinois, and raised in Catlin, Illinois. He received his BA in English from Northwestern University, MA from the University of Chicago, and his Ph.D. from New York University. He spent 1974-5 in Germany as a Fulbright Lecturer in American Literature, and now teaches at Oakton Community College in Des Plaines, Illinois.

Koenig's poems have recently appeared in the anthology *Blood to Remember: American Poets on the Holocaust* (1991). *The Ladder of Memory* is his second full-length book of poems. Recent honors include The Salute to the Arts Poetry Prize (1985) and The Friends of Literature Poetry Book Award (1989) for his first book of poems, *Green Whistle*.